Snowy oil drums at an airport.

ALASKA

in pictures

Prepared by JAMES NACH

VISUAL
GEOGRAPHY
SERIES

STERLING
PUBLISHING CO., INC. NEW YORK

Oak Tree Press Co., Ltd.
London & Sydney

VISUAL GEOGRAPHY SERIES

Many of the mountain-rimmed indentations of the coast of southeast Alaska rival the fiords of Norway in scenic beauty. This view of Rudyerd Bay is typical of the scenery in Tongass National Forest, much of which can be viewed from the decks of steamers and ferries navigating the Inside Passage.

PICTURE CREDITS

The publishers wish to thank the following for the use of the photographs in this book: Alaska Airlines; Alaska Steamship Company; Alaska Travel Division, Department of Economic Development and Planning; Alaska Visitors Association; Camp Denali Inc.; Caterpillar Tractor Co.; Humble Oil and Refining Co.; Pan American World Airways; Standard Oil Co. (N.J.); U.S. Air Force; U.S. Army; U.S. Fish and Wildlife Service; U.S. Forest Service; U.S. Public Health Service.

Russian churches at Unalaska are reminders of the days when Alaska belonged to Czarist Russia.

CONTENTS

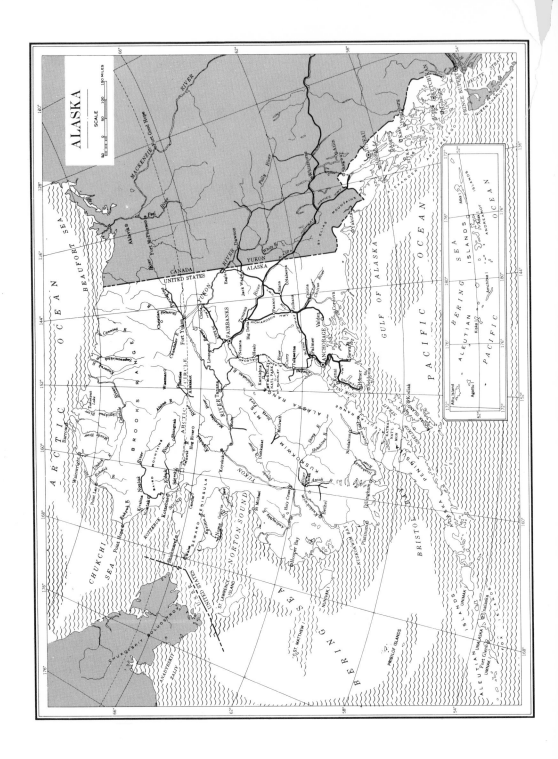

The Alaskan flag, adopted in 1927, was the design of a 13-year-old boy. The eight gold stars on a blue field are arranged to form the Great Bear constellation and the North Star. The blue represents the sky, the sea and the lakes, the gold stands for the wealth in Alaska's hills and streams.

I. HISTORY AND GOVERNMENT

Although its recorded history began little more than two centuries ago with the coming of European explorers, Alaska played an important rôle in the prehistoric development of the western hemisphere. At some distant time in the past, ancestors of the Indians crossed from extreme northeast Asia across a land bridge to Alaska. From there, Indian tribes spread throughout North and South America. The present Athabaskans of interior Alaska are closely related to two well-known tribes of Indians in the states of Arizona and New Mexico, the Apaches and the Navajos.

RUSSIAN AMERICA

While knowledge of the temperate areas of the globe had increased rapidly by the early 18th century, scarcely anything was known about the Pacific coastal region which lay north of the Spanish missions in California. No one was certain whether North America and Asia were or were not actually joined together some place far to the north, or whether islands studded the uncharted waters of the ocean. A final answer to the mystery did not come from explorers representing Spain, Britain, or France—nations

5

At one time Chief Shakes' Community House at Wrangell served as winter home for the fierce Stikine tribe of Tlingit Indians. During summers, Tlingit families went off to their personal fishing grounds. Before the coming of the Russians, the Tlingits usually sacrificed slaves to commemorate the building of a new home. This community house now serves as a museum for visitors to the southeast Alaska town, and contains an excellent collection of Tlingit tools and art objects.

that had staked claims to large parts of North America with the discovery of the new world. Instead, the riddle was solved by explorers from the east, from Russia.

Just as the United States of America was to begin expanding rapidly westward during the 19th century, Russia had begun an *eastward* movement across Siberia over 200 years before. By the opening of the 18th century, Russian traders and explorers had reached the Pacific coast, and interest grew in discovering what was beyond the horizon. Peter the Great, Czar of Russia, commissioned Vitus Bering, a Russian naval officer of Danish birth, to explore the blank space on the world map. Setting out from St. Petersburg (now Leningrad) in 1725, Bering and his party traversed the Siberian

wilderness and reached the Pacific in 1727. The next year, after having built a ship, Bering set sail in a northeasterly direction. On August 8, 1728, he discovered St. Lawrence Island, now part of the State of Alaska, and named it. Bering next headed north along the Siberian coast until the land suddenly fell away to the east. He then returned to the Siberian base from which he had set out. Bering had discovered the eastern limit of Asia, but the North American coast, hidden by fog, remained unseen. The strait through which Bering sailed is now named in tribute to him.

In 1741, Bering set sail once again, this time with two ships. Separated by a storm, the ship commanded by Bering's lieutenant, Alexei Chirikof, sighted the coast of southeast Alaska on July 15, 1741. The next day, 18,000-foot Mt. St. Elias came into view from Bering's boat. The Russian captains landed for no more than a few hours in Alaska; in fact, Chirikof lost a landing party to hostile Tlingit Indians. Scurvy broke out on the return journey, and Bering and many others perished. However, the survivors of Bering's second expedition brought back to European Russia the news of Alaska's discovery and of the sea otter and other valuable fur-bearing animals.

Soon the *promyshlenniki,* as the tough, ruthless Russian trader-hunters were called, crossed to the Aleutian Islands and the Alaskan mainland. The peaceful Aleuts were enslaved by the Russian hunters. The sea otter was nearly wiped out by the *promyshlenniki,* who shipped the hides back to St. Petersburg and Moscow where the animal's brown-black fur was prized by the wealthy. One of the traders, Gregor Shelikof, founded the first Russian settlement in North America on Kodiak Island in 1784.

Fifteen years later, disturbed by reports of the fierce rivalry for furs among the various Russian trading groups and news of how the Aleuts had suffered at the hands of the *promyshlenniki,* the Czar ordered the founding of the Russian America Company to handle the commerce (and government) of Alaska.

The Russian discovery of Alaska attracted the interest of other governments. In the last quarter of the 18th century, Spain, Britain and France sent ships to explore the coast of Russian America, as Alaska was then called. Many geographical place names testify to the visits of these foreign vessels. The great English sea captain, James Cook, searching the coast of Alaska in 1778 for an entrance to the long-sought northwest passage (which Frobisher, Davis, Hudson and other English explorers had tried to find from the eastern side of North America) sailed into a long, narrow body of water but was forced to "turn again" when the water came to an end. It is now known as the Turnagain Arm of Cook

The town of Kodiak nestles on the narrow strip of flat land between the sea and the hills on Kodiak Island. Canning of salmon and of Alaska king crab meat are the town's most important industries. Huge waves caused by the 1964 earthquake destroyed much of Kodiak's waterfront. The famed Kodiak brown bear, largest meat-eating animal in the world, roams the more remote parts of the 100-mile-long island.

Abraham Lincoln, who was President of the United States while Alaska was still a Russian possession, was not neglected by Tlingit totem carvers. This likeness is now in a Juneau museum.

of nearly a thousand Russian hunters and Aleuts and a Russian warship. The Indians fought off the Russians until their ammunition ran out and then retreated, leaving Baranof in control. A fortified town, Sitka, was built and soon became the headquarters for Russian activities in North America.

Under Baranof and his successors, Sitka developed into an important town, complete with sawmills, foundries, schools, even formal balls. However, Russian America was not as profitable to the mother country in the 19th century as it had been before. Many of the valuable fur-bearing animals had been nearly wiped out by unrestricted hunting. While the Russian government was losing interest in its distant possession in North America, another government (or, more accurately, another trading company) was slowly forcing its way into Russian America. Formed in 1670, the English-owned Hudson's Bay Company had made its

Graders widening the Richardson Highway in a 1954 reconstruction project. The highway, connecting Valdez on the southern coast with Fairbanks, is now paved over its entire length (as are most of Alaska's main roads). Snow-ploughs keep the Richardson Highway open throughout the winter.

Inlet. Disenchantment Bay marks the place where Malaspina, a Spanish captain, found a similar dead end. Valdez, one of the state's more important towns, has a name of Spanish origin.

Under the capable direction of Alexander Baranof, general manager of the Russian America Company, a new settlement was made on what is now named Baranof Island for the purpose of finding a fortune in furs in southeast Alaska. However, the Tlingit Indians, aware of the danger to their way of life in the coming of the Russians, overran the post and massacred most of the inhabitants in 1802. Two years later, Baranof returned to the island with a force

Baranof Island, on which Alaska's former capital, Sitka, is located, is distinguished by its rough topography. It is a land of thick forests, steep slopes, and mountain-ringed lakes.

influence felt throughout Canada by the 19th century. Only Russian America stood between the Company and the northern Pacific Ocean. A naval incident between British and Russian

Sitka was the last capital of Russian America. This replica of the original wooden blockhouse was built at the site of the old Russian fort near the town.

The region around Mt. St. Elias (18,008 feet), highest point on the border between the United States and Canada, is an expanse of huge ice fields and glaciers. Here, at Icy Bay, glaciers have spread out over hundreds of square miles of low-lying land in front of the mountains—a rare sight outside of polar regions. (Icy Bay is at the same latitude as Oslo, Norway, and Leningrad, in the Soviet Union.)

ships in Alaskan waters enabled Britain to pressure Russia into leasing the mainland of southeast Alaska to the Hudson's Bay Company beginning in 1839. By the mid-19th century, Russia began to fear that the British were becoming more interested in outright ownership of Alaska than in leasing arrangements. Already, Hudson's Bay Company agents had begun fur trading along the Yukon River far beyond the Canadian boundary. In order to forestall a British seizure of Alaska, the Russian government decided to sell the territory. The likeliest purchaser was the United States, which had been on friendly terms with Czarist Russia during the American Civil War.

"SEWARD'S FOLLY"

The Russian representative sent to Washington to negotiate the sale of Russian America, Baron Stoeckl, was able to convince Secretary of State William Seward and President Andrew Johnson that the U.S. should purchase the territory for $7,200,000. A treaty was concluded at 4 A.M. on March 30, 1867.

However, the United States Congress was far less enthusiastic about the purchase of Russian America than Seward. Only after some intensive political manoeuvring did the Senate approve the treaty, as required by the U.S. Constitution, and it did so by a margin of only two votes. During the debate in the Senate, Senator Charles Sumner of Massachusetts proposed that "Alaska," an Aleut name meaning "great land," be substituted for "Russian America." On October 18, 1867, a ceremony was held at Sitka marking the formal transfer of Alaska from Russia to the United States. Many people at the ceremony believed a new—and prosperous—era was beginning, but they were soon disappointed. The U.S. Congress was, at best, uninterested in the new acquisition. Many legislators had absolutely no knowledge of the value of Alaska; they assumed the territory consisted of several hundred thousand square miles of ice and frozen ground peopled by a few Eskimos and polar bears. Many nicknames were given Alaska: "Seward's Folly," "Icebergia," "Polaria," and "the icebox" (among others). The House of Representatives thought the purchase was such a waste of money that funds to pay the Russian Government were not voted until July, 1868.

PRE-GOLD-RUSH ERA

During the first decades of U.S. ownership, Alaska remained forgotten and neglected by the Government. From 1867 to 1884 it was impossible to open any land to settlement or development since there were no laws to secure land claims. However, since furs were the only product that Congress thought Alaska capable of producing, the Government did grant a private firm exclusive seal-hunting rights in the Pribilof Islands. At first the U.S. Army was placed in charge of Alaska, but the few troops that had been stationed at Sitka were withdrawn in 1877 (to fight in an Indian war in the western United States). Alaska then passed into the hands of the Treasury Department, which provided so little protection for the citizens of Sitka that they had to call in a British warship stationed in Canadian waters to protect them in 1879. The Navy Department—in the person of

Despite their suffering at the hands of early Russian fur hunters and adventurers, many Aleuts still adhere to the Russian Orthodox religion. Here, a Russian Orthodox priest on St. Paul Island marries an Aleut couple.

From the time of the spring break-up of ice on the Yukon and other large rivers of Alaska and Yukon Territory until the rivers froze over in autumn, sternwheeler steamboats carried passengers and cargo up- and down-stream. After World War II, aircraft and an expanded network of roads took away most of the sternwheelers' business and the last of them have been hauled up on to dry land for good.

The Casement is one of many large glaciers in Glacier Bay National Monument, a 3,600-square-mile preserve located about 100 miles northwest of Juneau. Changes in climate cause glaciers to retreat and advance. The nearby Muir Glacier retreated eight miles between 1899 and 1913.

The route to the Klondike gold fields was strewn with hardship. Some prospectors were wealthy enough to hire dogs to haul their heavily laden sleds; others pulled their own. Here, miners push a sled up a crude log ramp nicknamed Jacob's Ladder.

the commander of Navy ships anchored at Sitka—became the next guardian of Alaska.

In 1884, Congress finally created a civil government for Alaska by providing for the appointment of a governor. However, instead of drawing up laws suited to Alaska, Congress gave Alaska the law code of Oregon. At the time, Oregon was a settled state and Alaska, almost a complete wilderness. At the time, the population of Alaska numbered about 34,000, of whom only one or two thousand were whites, many of them living at the temporary capital of Sitka. The remainder were Eskimos, Aleuts, and Indians. The governor in Sitka had little idea of what was happening in the rest of Alaska since the government provided him with little money.

GOLD!

The happening which was to change abruptly the course of neglected Alaska's development did not even occur on Alaskan territory. In the summer of 1896, gold was discovered along a tributary of the Klondike River in the Canadian Yukon. While gold had previously been discovered at Juneau and other places in Alaska, richness of the new find attracted thousands of U.S. fortune-hunters to come over the next few years.

There were two main routes to the Klondike gold fields. One, the longer, was to go up the Yukon River by steamboat. The other was to go up the Inside Passage to Skagway and then to cross over the mountains to the Klondike.

13

An old prospector pans for gold at Nome. He is looking for "color," the yellowish flakes of gold that will indicate to him that he is panning gold-bearing gravel. By shaking the pan, the miner causes the gold particles to settle to the bottom, while the lighter rocks and dirt are washed away.

With the gold fever in the Klondike subsiding, reports of gold on the beaches at Nome set off a new stampede in 1900. Profit-hungry transportation companies attracted thousands of fortune hunters from all over the United States by distributing advertisements claiming that miners were making $300 per day with ease and that $500 gold nuggets were strewn over the beach. Unfortunately, those who came to Nome found very little gold. Instead of fortunes for all, there were high prices, violence in the muddy streets, and epidemics of typhoid fever and smallpox.

Many ill-equipped miners perished on the second route during the severe winters. Of those who arrived at the Klondike gold fields, a few made fortunes, but most went away poorer than when they arrived. Many miners drifted down the Yukon River into Alaska. New discoveries of gold at Fairbanks, Nome and other locations attracted even more miners from the United States. For the first time, the Government was prodded into aiding in the development of Alaska. Some surveys were made, a few lighthouses were built, and plans were made to build a road from Valdez, on the Gulf of Alaska, to the interior—the first long road ever built in Alaska (today known as the Richardson Highway).

ALASKA AS A TERRITORY

Alaska's population grew rapidly, and the 1900 census recorded 63,592 people, of which more than half were white. Under a 1906 act of Congress, Alaska was empowered to elect a non-voting delegate to Congress. In 1912, the incorporated Territory of Alaska was created. A two-house legislature was established to convene biennially at the capital, Juneau, and the first territorial legislature met in 1913.

Alaska, as a Territory, had a government that was part local and part federal. The Federal Government was represented in Alaska by the Governor, who was appointed by the President of the United States, with the consent of the

Like a procession of ants, prospectors struggle up the ice- and snow-clad slopes of Chilkoot Pass, leading to Canada's Yukon and the Klondike. Canadian authorities required prospectors to bring adequate supplies of food with them in order to prevent starvation in the gold camps. Snowslides were an ever-present danger; several hundred prospectors were killed by one during the spring of 1898. The tripods are part of an aerial tramway which carried the supplies of those who could afford the service.

Fairbanks (population 13,311 in 1960) is Alaska's second largest city. Like many other Alaskan towns, Fairbanks owes its existence to the gold rush at the turn of the century. In September, 1902, a miner named Felix Pedro discovered gold in a creek on the site of the present city. Today, modern buildings are rapidly displacing the last log cabins of the early gold prospectors. The Chena is the river flowing through the city.

Members of the U.S. Army Corps of Engineers prepare to rescue a bulldozer stuck in the mud during the construction of the Alaska Highway. Work began in March, 1942, and the road was officially opened eight months later. Aside from the difficulties involved in building a road through hundreds of miles of wilderness, the Engineers had to endure sub-zero temperatures during the winter months, and mud and mosquitoes during the summer.

In 1925, relays of dog teams rushed serum from Nanana (50 miles from Fairbanks) across 650 miles of wilderness to Nome, which had been struck by a diphtheria epidemic. Although aircraft and other forms of modern transport have reduced the need for dog teams, they are still used—both for business and sport. Here, two teams can be seen participating in a race. The most important races are held during the Anchorage Fur Rendezvous (February) and the Fairbanks Ice Carnival (March).

Senate, for a four-year term. The Territorial Government had executive and legislative divisions only; the Alaska judiciary was federal. There was no county form of government, and the Territory was divided into four judicial divisions, regardless of population.

During the first decades of the 20th century, great controversies raged as to how Alaska's natural resources should be developed. Large mining and business groups demanded that the Government turn over much of Alaska's resources for their private development. Most Alaskans, however, felt that the Territory's resources should be developed to benefit the

people of Alaska as well as wealthy investors who lived thousands of miles away. As a result, conservation-minded President Theodore Roosevelt ordered several valuable coal deposits withdrawn from private development.

The tendency of sometimes ill-informed officials in Washington to make far-reaching decisions on the use of Alaskan resources often had adverse effects. Unable to obtain cheap fuel, several companies abandoned plans to build railways linking the coastal towns of Valdez and Seward with the interior. Realizing the importance of a railway connection with the coast for the development of the economy of interior

Alaska, the U.S. Government, between 1915 and 1923, built the Alaska Railroad, which runs from Seward to Fairbanks. One of the construction camps along the rail line became known as Anchorage. It is now the largest and most important city in the state.

During the 1920's the pace of Alaska's growth slowed. In fact, the population of the Territory actually declined. Many left because they found Alaska was not, after all, a place to make "easy money." Unsympathetic members of Congress, determined not to "waste" money on a "worthless" land (although Alaska had by then produced minerals valued at more than a hundred times the $7.2 million purchase price), reduced the amount previously made available for exploration, research and development to practically nothing. They also forced the Department of the Interior to nearly double fares on the Alaska Railroad and to impose tolls on goods sent to the interior via the Richardson Highway.

Under the Administration of President Franklin D. Roosevelt, the Federal Government somewhat increased its activites in Alaska. The best-known Government project during this period was the resettlement of about 200 poverty-stricken farmers from the states of Minnesota, Michigan, and Wisconsin in the fertile Matanuska Valley north of Anchorage. Also benefiting Alaska was the increase in the price paid for gold by the U.S. Treasury (a step to help end the international financial depression of the 1930's). The higher price made it more profitable to mine gold, and many Alaskan gold-mining operations that had been forced to shut down, re-opened. By the end of 1939 the population of the Territory had increased to over 72,000.

Long desired by many Alaskans, the Alaska (Alcan) Highway was not built until after the United States had entered World War II. Alaska's only road connection with the lower 48 states, the highway begins at Dawson Creek, British Columbia, and runs northwestward through Canada's Yukon Territory and on into Alaska where it joins the Alaska road system at Big Delta—a distance of 1,422 miles. The Alaskan section of the road has now been paved; the Canadian section remains mostly gravel-surfaced.

United States Army troops lower themselves by rope on to the Eklutna Glacier (near Anchorage) during a training exercise. They will be ready to ski away on landing. On his back each man carries a pack, a rifle, and a pair of snowshoes. It is early June, yet winter still prevails in the mountains.

WARTIME

Before World War II, most people thought of Alaska as an isolated and unimportant U.S. possession. After the Japanese attack on Pearl Harbor in December, 1941, civilian and military planners suddenly came to realize the importance of Alaska's location, for the shortest route to Japan from the western United States passes just south of the Aleutian Islands. The Japanese seizure of Attu and Kiska Islands in 1942

19

Soldiers garbed in white camouflage advance against an imaginary foe during winter manoeuvres at Fort Richardson. An armed personnel carrier follows them through the snow. "General winter" has sometimes been the "victor" in training exercises held in temperatures which often drop below −50° F.

only served to point up Alaska's strategic position. As late as 1937, the Army garrison in Alaska numbered only 298 men (all stationed at the foot of the old trails to the Canadian Klondike). With the coming of war, tens of thousands of troops were sent to the Territory, military installations were built and the Alaska Highway was carved out of the northern wilderness—Alaska's first land connection with the "outside," the lower 48 states. When the war ended, many of those who had served in the armed forces in Alaska decided to make the Territory their permanent home.

American troops prepare to fire a mortar shell during the fighting on Attu Island. For its size, the campaign to drive the Japanese from the Aleutians was one of World War II's bloodiest. Note the heavy clothing worn by the soldiers to protect themselves from the inhospitable climate.

The Aleutian Islands, a part of Alaska stretching far from the mainland out into the Pacific Ocean, are treeless and virtually uninhabited. In 1942 the Japanese seized two of the most distant islands, Attu and Kiska, but one year later the United States Army drove out the invaders. Here, soldiers wade ashore on to Attu Island.

Should a rocket attack be launched against North America from across the Arctic Ocean, it would be instantly detected by this Ballistic Missile Early Warning System (BMEWS) station at Clear, Alaska, and by other stations located in Greenland and England.

A supersonic jet fighter roars off the runway at Elmendorf Air Force Base, near Anchorage. Fighter-interceptor squadrons stationed in Alaska are on round-the-clock alert and ready to defend North America against an air attack.

THE 49th STATE

Many Alaskans had long advocated statehood for the Territory. As early as 1916, a bill was introduced into Congress proposing statehood for Alaska. However, before World War II, the demands of Alaskans to have their homeland made the 49th state fell largely on deaf ears. Furthermore, owners of the profitable salmon canneries and larger mining operations preferred to keep Alaska a territory since they feared that statehood might bring restrictions on their business. As the population of Alaska increased, the influence of the large fish-canning and mining interests decreased. In 1949 and 1951, the Territorial Legislature enacted a number of revenue laws which, for the first time in Alaska's history, constituted a comprehensive tax structure to provide funds for

schools, hospitals, roads and other needs of Alaskans. Under a new law, salmon canners were made to pay a tax based on the value—rather than amount — of salmon packed.

In Alaska sentiment for becoming a state was growing. In 1956, a special convention drew up a constitution for the future State of Alaska. Meanwhile, in Washington, many members of Congress desired to put an end to what they believed was a disgrace to the United States, the "taxation without representation" to which Alaskans were subjected. On June 25, 1958, Congress voted statehood for Alaska. The decision was overwhelmingly approved by Alaskan voters in a special referendum, and on January 3, 1959, Alaska was proclaimed the 49th state of the Union by President Dwight D. Eisenhower.

STATE GOVERNMENT

The structure of the state government is similar to that of other states. The Governor, elected for a four-year term, is head of the executive branch. The Legislature consists of a 20-member Senate and a 40-member House. Government and politics in Alaska do have differences that distinguish them from those in other states. For instance, the Upper Yukon Election District (one of 24 into which the state is divided) has an area of 86,045 square miles (larger than 40 of the states in the Union), but has a population of only 1,619. Indians and Eskimos also participate in Alaskan government. An Eskimo from the village of Unalakleet was president of Alaska's first State Senate, and other Eskimos and Indians have served in the Legislature and as local officials.

Juneau, the capital of Alaska, is 1,033 miles northwest of Seattle, Washington. Situated on the Gastineau Channel, it is a lumber and fishing base and a transportation crossroad. With a population of 6,797 (1960), it has schools, hospitals, television and radio stations, and a daily and weekly newspaper. The city is named after Joe Juneau, a gold prospector who with a partner discovered gold on the site of the city in 1880.

23

Because of Alaska's high northern latitude, the length of day varies greatly between summer and winter. For example, on December 21 at Fairbanks the sun rises at 9:58 A.M. and sets at 1:40 P.M.; on June 21 it rises at 12:57 A.M. and sets at 11:48 P.M. The photograph, with exposure made at 20-minute intervals, shows the course of the sun in December.

Sunset falls on Mount McKinley National Park. A moose wades in Wonder Lake in search of a meal of aquatic plants. Mount McKinley rises in the background.

Mt. McKinley, highest mountain in North America, has two peaks. The South Peak (left, rear) is the true summit with an altitude of 20,320 feet. Two miles away (right) is the North Peak, 850 feet lower. The ascent of the mountain is not for amateur mountaineers. However, in 1910, two gold prospectors equipped with little more than bamboo poles reached the top of the North Peak. Why they chose the lower peak is unknown, but they may have felt they could be more easily seen by their friends (using telescopes) 150 miles away in Fairbanks. Unfortunately, they were neither seen nor believed, but three years later the first party to climb the South Peak sighted a bamboo pole at the summit of the North Peak.

2. THE LAND

The most striking fact about Alaska is its huge size. With a total area of 586,400 square miles, Alaska is well over twice the size of Texas, the next largest state. (Compared with Western Europe, Alaska is about the size of the United Kingdom, France, West Germany, and Spain *combined.*)

Alaska is the largest peninsula of the North American continent. On the east, the state has a land boundary with Canada that runs south from the Arctic Ocean along the 141st meridian west, to a point not far from the Gulf of Alaska.

From there, the boundary twists through

A map of Alaska superimposed on a map of the lower 48 states shows the great size and geographical extent of the state. The distance from Ketchikan in southeast Alaska to Attu Island in the Aleutians is as great as the distance from South Carolina to California. Alaskans are well aware that their state is more than twice the size of Texas.

some of the most mountainous terrain in North America, separating Alaska's narrow "Panhandle" from the Canadian province of British Columbia. This part of the international frontier was not fixed until 1903. Before that time, Canada had claimed that the boundary lay 10 marine leagues from the coast, while the United States claimed that the 10 marine leagues should be measured from the heads of the many inlets in the coast. In 1903, a tribunal of three Americans, two Canadians, and the Lord Chief Justice of Britain met to discuss the dispute. Lord Alverstone, the British representative, sided with the Americans, and the Canadian view was outvoted four to two.

Alaska borders on no other state. Its southernmost point, not far from the "salmon capital" of the state, Ketchikan, is separated from the lower 48 states by British Columbia.

The 49th state includes both the northernmost and the westernmost points in the United States within its boundaries. Point Barrow (71° 23′ north latitude) on the Arctic Ocean is farthest north; Attu Island in the Aleutians is farther west (172° 27′ east longitude) than any point in Hawaii. Because several of the Aleutian Islands are beyond the 180th meridian, the International Date Line, separating today from tomorrow, makes a detour around the Aleutians so that they can all be included in one of Alaska's four time zones.

The western tip of the Seward Peninsula is but 55 miles from Soviet Siberia, lying across the Bering Strait. Midway in the strait are the Diomede Islands. Little Diomede is part of Alaska; Big Diomede, 2½ miles away, is owned by the Soviet Union. Because the International Date Line runs between the two islands, residents of Little Diomede can watch the people of Big Diomede go about their lives the next day.

Cows graze peacefully in a meadow not far from the snout of the Mendenhall Glacier. They have no need to fear being buried under a sheet of ice, for the glacier has been receding in recent decades. However, owing to heavier snowfalls in the mountains in recent years, scientists predict that the Mendenhall Glaciers will begin advancing towards the end of the 20th century.

The Alaska Railroad's main line runs from Seward, on the Gulf of Alaska, northward to Anchorage and Fairbanks, a total distance of 470 miles. It is the only railway in the United States owned and operated by the Federal Government. Moose and other animals are frequently seen from the trains. At one point, the tracks come within 46 miles of Mt. McKinley.

Many large Alaskan towns, mainly in the southeastern part of the state, are not connected with the central Alaskan road system. In order to improve Alaska's transport network, the state has put into operation a fleet of modern ferries. The most important route has its southern terminus at Prince Rupert, British Columbia (Canada), and serves Ketchikan, Wrangell, Petersburg, Sitka, Juneau, Haines, and Skagway. By taking the ferry up the Inside Passage, motorists can save 600 miles of driving over the Alaska (Alcan) Highway.

REGIONS

Alaska may be roughly divided into four major regions. The first of these, the Pacific Mountain Region consists of a series of mountain ranges paralleling the Pacific coast at various distances from the ocean. In the Panhandle region, the Coast Mountains, extending northward from British Columbia, pass behind Juneau and farther northward form the mountain barrier that caused so much hardship for gold seekers heading for the Klondike at the turn of the century. Parallel to the Coast

Mountains are several lower ranges whose higher portions form the hundreds of islands of the Alexander Archipelago. Sitka, the old capital of Alaska, is located on Baranof Island, a part of the archipelago.

Farther up the coast of the Gulf of Alaska are the summits of the ice-clad St. Elias Mountains and Chugach Mountains. Several of the peaks in these ranges and in the Wrangell Mountains to the north are taller than Mt. Whitney in California, highest peak in the other 49 states, but not as tall as Mt. McKinley. Also present are some of the largest glaciers and ice fields outside of polar areas.

Extending southwest from the Anchorage area are more mountains, the Aleutian Range and the Kenai Mountains (which disappear under the ocean and one later reappears as Kodiak Island). Many of the peaks of the Aleutian Range, which extends down the Alaska Peninsula and is responsible for the Aleutian Island chain, are active volcanoes. Katmai National Monument, largest unit in the National Park System, contains the Novarupta volcano. In 1912, Novarupta literally blew its top. A gigantic explosion cast an estimated two cubic miles of rock and ash into the sky. Kodiak Island was buried under a foot of ash, while other ash from the blast found its way into the stratosphere and caused brilliant sunsets in the north-

Mt. Alyeska's ski slopes glisten in the winter sun. The resort, located in Chugach National Forest, can easily be reached from Anchorage, about 40 miles away by road. A chair lift carries skiers to the top of the slopes. In summer, the lift operates for the benefit of tourists.

The laying of oil and gas pipelines is the necessary result of Alaska's growing population and the requirements of the military establishment. Here, a construction crew lowers a section of fuel pipeline into position in interior Alaska. One of the state's newest pipelines brings natural gas to Anchorage from wells on the Kenai Peninsula.

Good soil and 18 hours of summer sunshine daily helped to produce this giant cabbage, a product of the Matanuska Valley, to the north of Anchorage. The long hours of daylight during the summer make up, to some extent, for the short growing season.

ern hemisphere for many months. A side effect of the blast was the formation of the Valley of Ten Thousand Smokes (now inactive), discovered by a National Geographic Society (U.S.) expedition in 1916.

It should not be thought that the Pacific Mountain Region is composed of nothing but ice, rock, and volcanoes. Some of the best commercial forests in the United States are located in southeast Alaska. In other areas there are broad river valleys and open spaces, although mountains are always in sight. Parts of the Kenai Peninsula and the Matanuska Valley offer the best farming land in the state. Where valleys are below sea level, the ocean has formed long inlets which provide safe ports for shipping. Resurrection Bay, at whose head Seward, Alaska's most important port, is located, is a good example.

About 130 miles north of Anchorage is the heart of the Alaska Range, which separates the Pacific Mountain Region from the Yukon Plateau. The Alaska Range includes the highest peak in North America, Mt. McKinley (20,320 feet). North of the Alaska Range the

Horseshoe Lake stands at the eastern edge of Mt. McKinley National Park, one of the largest units in the national park system. Although dominated by Mt. McKinley, the park has many other worthy scenic attractions. Formerly reachable only by railway or plane, Mt. McKinley Park is now linked with the state highway network.

Anchorage International Airport is one of the principal airfields of the world. There is frequent service to the "outside" (the Alaskan nickname for the lower 48 states) and to most Alaskan towns. Anchorage is a stopping place for planes flying the great circle route to the Orient and for others flying the "over the pole" route to Europe from the western United States.

Here is what the airport tower in Anchorage looked like immediately after the 1964 earthquake.

Those who parked their cars on the left side of Fourth Avenue in Anchorage just before the 1964 earthquake found them where they were left. However, on the right side of the street, the cars, pavement, roadway and shops had dropped 15 feet. In a matter of seconds the earthquake destroyed millions of dollars of property; however, the toll of dead and injured was relatively light.

Ketchikan, population 6,483, is the southernmost city in Alaska and is the first port of call for north-bound ferries and steamers. Fishing and lumbering are the two most important commercial activities of the region. In fact, Ketchikan canneries process more salmon than any other in the world.

terrain consists of a vast area of low plateaus and hills. Alaska's two most important rivers, the Yukon and the Kuskokwim, drain interior Alaska, and both streams empty into the Bering Sea. Forests of relatively small white spruce, birch, and poplar crowd the river valleys and low-lying sections of the interior. Fairbanks is the most important town in the region.

North of the Arctic Circle, the Brooks Range crosses Alaska from east to west. The Arctic Slope consists of land descending gradually from the northern foothills of the Brooks Range to the lowland areas bordering on the Arctic Ocean. It is a land of wolves, caribou and Eskimos. There are no trees, only tundra, a layer of vegetation covering the frozen soil which is composed of hardy grasses and shrub willows. In summer, innumerable ponds and small lakes dot the countryside. The largest settlement in the region is Barrow, which is also the northernmost town in the U.S.

Northern Lights glow over Fairbanks.

This sheer cliff, rugged but beautiful, rises sharply from the shores of Behm Canal in the Tongass National Forest.

CLIMATE

When Alaska was purchased by the U.S. a century ago, most people believed "Seward's Folly" to be a frozen wasteland. The belief that Alaska is a cold and inhospitable place still persists. Because of its great size, Alaska can boast no single climate to be found in all parts of the state. Because it is warmed by the Japanese current in the Pacific Ocean, southeast Alaska has a relatively mild climate. Juneau's average January temperature is 25.1° F. Summer temperatures in the Panhandle are cool but not cold—usually in the 50's and 60's. Rain, on which the forests thrive, is a frequent occurrence in southeast Alaska. Precipitation averages about 150 inches per year at Ketchikan. In the mountains, heavy snow falls throughout the year and feeds the great ice fields and glaciers for which Alaska is famous.

Farther north along the Pacific coast, winter temperatures become colder—but not cold enough to freeze over many ports. However, as one travels inland temperatures become colder in winter. Seward, on the Gulf of Alaska (Pacific Ocean), has an average January temperature of 22.4° F while Anchorage, at the head of Cook Inlet and less than 100 miles away, has a January average of 11.2°F. Precipitation also decreases in a similar manner. Seward averages 73.7 inches annually; Anchorage, only 14.32. Summer temperatures in the Anchorage vicinity are much like those in southeast Alaska.

North of the Alaska Range, the moderating effects of the ocean on temperature are not felt. The interior of the state has a climate similar to that of Montana, North Dakota, or Manitoba. Winters are extremely cold. Fairbank's average January temperature is a chilly −11.6°F, with a record low of −66°. However, snowfall is moderate (Fairbanks' average annual precipitation of 11.9 inches is less than one-third New York City's), and the harsh, wind-driven winter storms that frequently strike states from

Alaska is a land of contrasts. These twin glaciers—frozen rivers of ice—flow from ice fields high in the mountains to an arm of the ocean. The summer house (below) is located deep in the woods near Juneau. Moist air, blowing in from the Gulf of Alaska, is responsible for both the snow that feeds the coastal glaciers at their sources in the mountains and the heavy rainfall on which the forests of southeast Alaska thrive.

Humans are not Alaska's only salmon fishermen. Caring not at all for nets, hooks, lines and other necessities of human fishermen, Alaska brown bears skilfully catch salmon by swatting them from the water with a swipe of a paw. After a summer spent fattening themselves on salmon and berries, the bears will be ready for their long hibernation.

the Great Plains eastward to New England are unknown in interior Alaska. During summer, long hours of daylight are responsible for warm temperatures. Fort Yukon, located on the Yukon River just above the Arctic Circle, has had extremes of −78° in winter and 100° in summer.

Even though farther north, the Arctic coast of Alaska experiences slightly milder weather than the interior because of the nearness of the Arctic Ocean. Far from being a land of ice and snow drifts, Alaska's northernmost region is extremely dry. Barrow receives but 4.3 inches of precipitation per year on the average.

Much of the ground of Alaska north of the

Alaska Range is frozen solid all year for depths ranging from a few feet to 200 feet—a condition known as permafrost. In summer, there is some thawing, but if the top layer of mosses, shrubs and soil is removed, permafrost can usually be found near the surface of the earth. Because of permafrost, water cannot be readily absorbed into the ground, and in poorly drained areas this results in swampy conditions during the summer. When the vegetation insulating permafrost is removed, the frozen ground thaws in an uneven manner. Builders who construct homes on thawing permafrost risk cracked foundations. Wavy pavement on many Alaska roads also testifies to the dangers of building on permafrost.

FAUNA

Alaska is one of the world's great wildlife regions—both in the number and variety of its animals. Although found in other parts of North America, the moose, largest member of the deer family, reaches its greatest size in Alaska. Bull moose on the Kenai Peninsula often reach weights of over 1,400 pounds and grow six-foot antler spreads. Moose are vegetarians; they feed on the tender shoots of willow, aspen and birch, and during the summer, sometimes feed on underwater vegetation found in lakes. When the fall mating season comes, bull moose frequently lock antlers in violent struggles fought to determine "ownership" rights over a female moose. In winter, bull moose shed their antlers; a new set begins growing in April. Wolves and bears are the greatest enemies of the moose, frequently attacking the very young, the very old, and the unwary.

The giant Kodiak brown bear, largest meat-eating animal on earth, is the best-known of all Alaskan fauna. This bruin is closely related to the grizzly bear. Both brown and grizzly bears

This wolverine has just emerged from the water. The fur of the wolverine is frostproof, and Eskimos and other parka-wearers use it to trim the hoods of the garments. An inhabitant of mountain forests, the wolverine often attacks larger animals and breaks into cabins whose owners are away. It is the largest member of the weasel family.

The fur seals come ashore only in summer to breed and rear their young. The bull seal is surrounded by his harem and pups. Each mother seal knows instinctively which pup is her own and will have nothing to do with an orphan, which will be left to die.

37

The fearless musk ox was exterminated by hunters during the 19th century. In 1930, 34 of the animals were transported from Greenland to Fairbanks, and six years later the herd was released on Nunivak Island in the Bering Sea where it has thrived and increased, being protected by law from hunters' bullets. A full-grown musk ox weighs about 600 pounds—including its thick, shaggy coat.

A fox makes his rounds in Mount McKinley National Park. During the long winter, the park is all but deserted—except for wildlife and park rangers. Snow blocks the road, and winter travel must be by means of dog sled, snowmobile, or snow-shoes.

prefer to have nothing to do with man. They range over almost the entire state, living on a diet of berries, fish, small animals, and an occasional moose before going into their annual winter hibernation. Inhabiting the forested lowland areas of Alaska are the black bears, the familiar "highway bandits" often found begging tourists for food in parks in the United States and Canada. In Alaska, opportunities for roadside handouts are very limited, but woe to the Alaskan who does not bear-proof his cabin. Bears are experts at breaking and entering and think little of tearing apart a cabin if their sensitive noses detect the smell of a free meal inside. Black bears are not always black, but have different shades of fur—brown, cinnamon, and a rare blue bear found living near glaciers in southeast Alaska. White-coated polar bears live on the ice packs in the Arctic Ocean,

Moose like this furnish the winter's meat supply for hundreds of Alaskan families who store moose steaks in freezers—or outside, in nature's freezer. Largest member of the deer family, Alaska moose are found throughout most of the state. Bull moose often attain weights of three-quarters of a ton with antler spreads of over six feet.

The fur of sea otters, seen basking by the water here, is unmatched in fineness, density, durability, beauty and value. Because of it, they too were nearly exterminated, but now killing them is prohibited by law.

Dall sheep roam many of Alaska's higher mountain areas. These wild white sheep are prized trophies for hunters.

Murres, similar in appearance to penguins, are sea birds that return to the rocky islands each summer to rear their young.

gain their food supply from the sea, and are the only Alaskan bear that does not hibernate regularly. Eskimos hunt the polar bear, for the animal furnishes them with meat and material for warm clothing.

Ranging over much of Alaska's treeless tundra regions are caribou, members of the deer family closely related to the reindeer. In fact, caribou frequently cross-breed with reindeer. Caribou feed on slow-growing lichens and often migrate long distances in search of new food supplies. Both male and female caribou grow antlers.

Among the other large, native Alaskan animals are the graceful Dall mountain sheep, mountain goats and deer. The state also possesses a large number of smaller animals, many of which are valuable for their fur. They include beaver, foxes, mink, muskrat, lynx and weasel. Best-known of the state's predatory animals is the wolf, a close relative of the dog and one of the few wild animals to lead a true family life.

Alaska is the temporary or permanent home of a number of bird species. Each summer hundreds of thousands of ducks and geese migrate northward from winter homes in Mexico and the southern United States to nest in Alaska.

Some geese find the climatic variations within Alaska to their liking and do not fly beyond the borders of the state. Alaska's most important varieties of upland game birds are several types of ptarmigan and grouse. The state's most famous bird of prey is the bald eagle, the national bird of the United States which is in danger of dying out in the other states of the Union.

MAN AND WILDLIFE

Today, Alaska is the last great wilderness area in the United States. Whether it will remain so and whether wildlife will continue to thrive depends largely on the actions of man. The mass slaughter of sea otters and fur seals during the 18th and 19th centuries was a vivid demonstration of the impact of man on Alaskan wildlife. Present-day laws prohibit the unrestricted killing of most animals, but growing cities, farms and industries are having their effect. On Kodiak Island, for instance, cattle ranchers frequently shoot brown bears because the huge animals sometimes kill cattle. As the ranches expand, the number of Kodiak bears will probably decrease. Similarly, the construction of Rampart Dam and the resulting flooding of the Yukon Valley will destroy the home of large numbers of waterfowl, moose and other animals. Pressures are mounting in other areas to open wildlife sanctuaries to prospecting for petroleum and other minerals.

With proper management both wildlife and man can continue to exist side by side. However, when wildlife is endangered man sometimes tends to blame other causes when he himself is really at fault. Although hunting pressures and overgrazing of feeding grounds by imported reindeer are primarily responsible for the decline in numbers of caribou, wolves are usually blamed and bounties are paid to anyone killing a wolf. Salmon fishermen, faced with a reduced catch, are quick to point out that the Dolly Varden trout eats salmon eggs. However, the salmon thrived for countless centuries before fishermen began decimating them with nets and traps within the last 100 years.

Some of Alaska's most interesting animals are newcomers brought to the state by man. In 1928, 23 buffaloes were brought from Montana and released near Big Delta, Alaska. The herd has done so well that limited hunting is now necessary to control its size. Musk oxen were re-introduced into Alaska in 1930 after an absence of three-quarters of a century. A project is now under way to provide Eskimos with herds of musk oxen. The fine wool undercoating of the animal, known as qiviut, is of approximately the same quality as cashmere wool—and each musk ox yields as much of the valuable wool annually as 30 cashmere goats. It is hoped that Eskimos will be able to sell qiviut and items knitted from it as a means towards economic self-sufficiency. Other animals brought into Alaska in recent times are the reindeer and the wapiti (American elk).

No snakes of any kind are found in Alaska.

The world's largest and most valuable fur seal herd returns from its oceanic wintering ground to the Pribilof Islands every summer. Unrestricted hunting during the 19th century nearly exterminated the herd, but a treaty signed by the United States, Britain, Russia, and Japan in 1911 ended the slaughter and provided for controlled hunting under the auspices of the U.S. Government. With conservation measures in force the herd has increased to its former size—and the U.S. Government has made large profits from sales of seal skins.

Bustling Anchorage looks much like any other small American city. Heavy traffic and crowds of shoppers are a common sight on Fourth Avenue, the city's main street. Although heavily damaged by the violent 1964 earthquake, Anchorage has recovered rapidly and most damaged buildings have been repaired or replaced.

These Eskimos of Nunivak Island stand beside their hillside home. Many Eskimo homes are built into the hillside and then covered with sod. Well protected from the cold and wind, they are comfortable during the winter.

The Eskimo combines tradition with modern customs. Bubble gum and kayaks are both part of this Nunivak Island boy's life.

3. THE PEOPLE

Ever since Alaska was acquired by the United States in 1867, its citizens have been American citizens. As such they have been and are subject to the duties and obligations of citizenship, including service in the armed forces and the payment of federal income taxes. With the coming of statehood, Alaskans now have the right to elect Senators and Congressmen to represent their state in the United States' Congress.

In 1960, when the last census was taken, the population of Alaska was 226,167, including military personnel stationed in the state. Alaska is the most sparsely settled state in the Union with a population density of only 0.4 persons per square mile (compared to a density of 50.5 per square mile for the entire United

Mother pickles seal meat to provide food for the winter, and her daughter learns house-keeping, Eskimo-style.

43

When snow comes, these dogs will be harnessed to sleds. Eskimos use dog teams while hunting or for trips between villages. These dogs appear to be waiting eagerly for their dinner of raw fish.

While other American children are rolling Easter eggs on the lawn of the White House in Washington, Anchorage youngsters are hunting for eggs in the snow. The snow lasts until well into the spring.

States and 790 per square mile for England). Of the total population in 1960, 174,546 are white, while the remaining 51,621 includes 14,444 Indians and 28,637 Aleuts and Eskimos.

Alaska's population is concentrated in and around a few towns and cities. Anchorage, with a 1960 population of 44,237, is the largest city in the state. Thousands more live in nearby communities and at the military bases just north of the city, Elmendorf Air Force Base and Fort Richardson. Fairbanks, population 13,311, is the most important town in the interior. In the Panhandle region, the larger towns are the capital, Juneau (6,797), Ketchikan (6,483), and Sitka (3,237). All told, there are only seven communities in the entire state with a population exceeding 2,500. Many isolated settlements in the interior and along the coasts have only a few dozen inhabitants. However, some of the salmon-canning towns have variable populations. During the salmon runs, workers flock to the canneries from the surrounding villages; others are flown in on chartered aircraft from Washington, Oregon, and other states. When the packing season ends, the temporary population speedily vanishes.

Fishing through the ice is an art perfected by the Eskimos, and women are as proficient as men.

LIFE IN ALASKA

Alaskans of the mid-twentieth century have lives similar in many ways to Americans from other states. However, there are also some significant differences. In Anchorage, Fairbanks, and the other larger communities the muddy street and wooden pavement are a thing

Planes play a leading rôle in Alaskan life. Trips that formerly took days by land or boat can now be made in hours or minutes. Per capita ownership of aircraft is higher in Alaska than in any other state. Here, an amphibian is tied up alongside a dock at the fishing village of Baranof. Note the height of the pier in the background above the water. Twenty-foot tides are common along the twisting coastline of southeast Alaska.

Alaskan brown bear pelts make handsome trophies, but most people prefer to shoot with a camera.

Tlingit children learn about the customs of their ancestors from their grandfather.

Swimming in Alaska is not restricted to polar bears. Warm summer temperatures and long hours of daylight heat up the upper layers of lake water. However, deep divers may find swimming rather cool. These swimmers are enjoying the waters of Dredge Lake, 12 miles from Juneau. The Mendenhall Glacier is beyond the line of trees in the background.

Alaska's snow-covered mountains provide a skier's paradise. Here is Douglas Ski Bowl on Douglas Island, near Juneau. The mountains on the upper left are located on the Alaskan mainland.

47

Reindeer are not native to Alaska. A semi-domesticated relative of the caribou, the animal was first brought to Alaska in 1891 when the U.S. Department of the Interior imported 12 Siberian reindeer to provide a source of meat for the Eskimos. The original herd thrived and more of the animals were brought in, as were Laplanders who were hired to show the Eskimos how to care for reindeer. Today, the reindeer provides thousands of Eskimos with a supply of meat and skins (from which clothing is made).

of the past—parking meters and street lights are as commonplace there as in hundreds of other American towns. Schools provide Alaskan youngsters with an excellent education from the primary school level through university training (at the University of Alaska at College and the Alaska Methodist University at Anchorage). Radio and television stations and newspapers keep Alaskans informed of world and local events. In Anchorage, there are music festivals, motion picture theatres, night clubs, and other cultural diversions to suit every taste.

Yet many aspects of life in Alaska are unique. The wilderness is never far away, and most Alaskans are outdoor enthusiasts: hiking, sport fishing, hunting, skiing, mountain climbing, and photography among others. Alaskan cele-brations are in harmony with the surroundings. Dogsled races are an important part of the Anchorage Fur Rendezvous, a northern version of the New Orleans Mardi Gras. Seward holds an annual salmon-fishing derby and also sponsors a gruelling foot-race up and down nearby 3,022-foot Mt. Marathon to celebrate the Fourth of July.

Many people living "outside" are surprised by the high wages paid for work in Alaska. However, there is a simple explanation: high prices. Nearly all food and manufactured items must be brought in from other states. By the time goods reach isolated villages in the interior they are staggeringly expensive. Even in Anchorage, prices are considerably higher than in other states. The U.S. Government pays its employees 25 per cent higher wages than in other states to make up for the Alaskan cost of living.

Along with high prices, Alaskans have learned to take many things for granted such as cold winters with their short hours of daylight. Bush pilots regularly transport passengers and freight to and from the multitude of primitive airstrips in the interior. Many Alaskans use their own planes to visit friends and to go on errands to town in the manner that other Americans use the automobile. Informality and simple dress are the rule throughout the state. Although life in Alaska may not be as comfortable and easy as in other states, Alaskans are quite willing to continue living as they are—without air pollution, junk yards, and billboard-lined highways.

ESKIMOS

Alaska's native population is divided into three major groups: the Eskimos, the Aleuts, and the Indians. The best known and most numerous are the Eskimos who live mainly along the treeless Arctic coast and Bering Sea coast. Before the coming of the white man, the Eskimo lived a primitive—but happy—life, gaining his livelihood from hunting and fishing. Contrary to popular belief, Eskimos lived in igloos for only short periods, particularly while on hunting trips. Most lived in dwellings constructed of sod cut from the tundra. When the white man came, he brought with him new customs, new diseases and firearms. Many unscrupulous white men took advantage of the Eskimos. Tuberculosis and other diseases

The University of Alaska, located at College (near Fairbanks) is the farthest north university in North America. It is a land-grant college, owned by the State of Alaska. Research into the Northern Lights and other Arctic phenomena is carried on at the University. The varied exhibits in the University museum have attracted many visitors.

Mother walks; baby rides. Like children every-where, Eskimo youngsters are treated with great affection by their elders.

spread rapidly with lethal effect. With rifles bought from white traders, Eskimos were able to kill more meat-providing caribou than ever before, so many, in fact, that the caribou herds were seriously reduced in numbers.

Today, Eskimos are slowly being integrated into the way of life of their fellow American citizens. Eskimo children go to government schools, and many go on to work in the mining

Tall, gaily painted totem poles dot the Tlingit country in southeast Alaska. The intricately carved figures on the totems represent tribal laws, customs, and usages covering kinship, marriage, property and descent. Each Tlingit clan usually had its own distinctive totem symbols which were handed down from generation to generation in the same manner that coats of arms are.

The old Eskimo art of making both useful and decorative objects still survives despite the inroads made by mail-order catalogues. Here, a young Eskimo drills a hole in a piece of walrus-tusk ivory. The vice he is using is modern; the bowstring drill, traditional. Tourists visiting Alaska purchase many of the products of Eskimo craftsmanship.

The fireplaces in many Alaskan lodging places are living reminders of the days not long ago when the roads were trails and inns were few and far between. Tired travellers used to gather around fireplaces to swap stories of their trips and news from the different gold camps.

A group of Tlingit carvers work on a large totem with modern tools that their ancestors never knew. However, they will coat the finished totem pole with natural vegetable and mineral paints prepared according to age-old methods. Totem carving was a dying art throughout the first third of the 20th century, but during the 1930's the U.S. Forest Service and the Civilian Conservation Corps helped revive the art. At present there is a good market for the works of Indian carvers.

The now-abandoned Old Kasaan Village on Prince of Wales Island in Tongass National Forest was formerly occupied by Indians of the Haida tribe, who originally came from British Columbia, Canada. Old Kasaan and other Haida villages consisted of rows of frame houses built in clearings close to the shore. The Indians exercised considerable ingenuity in constructing their homes without the benefit of iron cutting tools and nails. However, when the white man came, the quality of Indian craftsmanship declined. Villages such as Old Kasaan were deserted for paying jobs at the newly built salmon canneries.

In order to visit his widely scattered patients, this U.S. Public Health Service doctor often uses a combination of old and new forms of transport. Here, he checks his dog team. In the background is his plane, which is fitted with skis to permit landings on snow.

and fishing industries or in other fields. However, Eskimos are proud of their traditional customs and skills, and many choose to live much as their ancestors did.

ALEUTS AND INDIANS

The Aleuts, a group of aborigines closely related to the Eskimos, and the Indians of Alaska have been more nearly assimilated into the "modern" way of life. About 500 Aleuts are employed in the Pribilof Island sealing operations. Thousands of Aleuts and Tlingit Indians work in the canneries during the salmon season. Unfortunately, many of the old customs are being lost—or are revived only for the tourist trade. One of the most interesting of the bygone customs was the Tlingit potlatch, a huge feast at which the host gained prestige by giving away everything he owned.

This little Eskimo girl seems more interested in the photographer and her doll than in the salmon fisherman's catch. However, the fisherman probably does not mind the lack of attention; he can look forward to several tasty meals.

The Eskimo family is a close-knit one. Age and youth live together in harmony. Here, an Eskimo girl, clad in a parka, performs a native dance. Men beat out the rhythm on drums.

This old Eskimo woman has seen many changes during her lifetime.

54

Western hemlock, Sitka spruce, and other evergreens thrive in the moist, relatively warm climate of southeastern Alaska. Here, rafts of logs float in front of a Ketchikan mill, which will soon turn them into wood pulp from which rayon and other products will be manufactured elsewhere.

4. THE ECONOMY

To date, Alaska's economy has been almost totally dependent on the state's vast wealth of natural resources. Compared to California, New York, and other important industrial states, Alaska has few manufacturing industries to speak of. Yet this does not mean that the state is "underdeveloped" in the sense that the so-called "emerging" nations of Asia, Africa, and Latin America are. As has been the case in New Zealand, the people of Alaska have forged a prosperous way of life for themselves without having to depend upon heavy manufacturing industries for their livelihood.

THE FISHING INDUSTRY

At present, the sea is Alaska's most valuable natural resource. The fishing industry employs about 30,000 people, a greater number than does any other commercial activity in the state. Taxes levied on fishing companies supply a large portion of revenues for the state government.

The salmon is by far the most important fish in Alaska's economy. Hatched in streams and lakes that are often hundreds of miles from the sea, young salmon travel down the rivers to the

ocean. After three to seven years at sea (depending upon the type of salmon, among which are the king, silver, sockeye, pink, and chum varieties), the mature salmon, guided by instinct, return to coastal waters, fight their way upstream (often leaping through rapids and waterfalls) until they reach the streams of their birth. There they spawn—and die.

Although Indians and bears had long feasted on protein- and vitamin-rich salmon meat, the Russians paid little attention to the potentialities of salmon fishing. In 1878, however, American investors opened Alaska's first salmon cannery. Other companies quickly followed suit, and in several places (Ketchikan, for example) towns grew up around the salmon canneries. Over the years more and more mechanized equipment was put into operation

Fishermen "purse a seine"—encircle a school of fish with a net—on Ernest Sound. During fish runs, lucky boat crews may make thousands of dollars apiece.

Salmon boats arrive at one of the state's many salmon canneries. During the salmon runs, which occur at different times in different parts of the state, the highly mechanized canneries work around the clock to clean, cook and can the catches of salmon.

to catch and can salmon. Today the salmon industry is a mainstay of Alaska's economy, providing many jobs and bringing in a large income.

Unfortunately, the salmon-fishing industry has not matched mechanization with conservation. As more efficient gear was put into use, fewer and fewer salmon escaped the fisherman's nets and traps to spawn. And each year, fewer and fewer salmon were caught. Profit-seeking salmon canners successfully defeated all attempts to pass effective laws to help conserve the salmon

supply. Not until one year after statehood did the Alaska Legislature gain control over the state's own fisheries. The efficient fish traps blocking the mouths of rivers were speedily outlawed and other regulations were passed, but it is still too early to tell whether the salmon runs will be permanently—and substantially—increased. There is, at present, considerable fear that Japanese and Russian ocean fishing fleets may be seriously depleting the salmon supply.

Alaska's streams are a delight to anglers. The state has a variety of rivers and creeks, ranging from the fast-falling streams of the Panhandle region to the slower-flowing water courses of the interior. Among the fish are several species of salmon and of trout, grayling, great northern pike, and inconnu. Here, a fisherman casts for salmon in Sweethart Creek, Tongass National Forest.

A gold dredge works its way up a creek bed near Fairbanks. The dredge floats on its own lake. Buckets mounted in front scoop up gold-bearing gravel. The gold is separated, later to be refined for sale, and the gravel is deposited in the rear of the dredge. Land worked over by a dredge is of little use for other purposes.

MINING

Gold mining, which once attracted thousands of fortune hunters to Alaska and produced so much wealth, is a declining industry in Alaska today. While production costs of gold mining have spiralled upward in the last three decades, the price of the metal has remained fixed by law at $35 per ounce. However, there are still a number of small placer mines in operation.

Very little of Alaska has been adequately searched for mineral resources. Thorough search of the state for useful minerals will take many years—possibly decades. So far, 31 of 33 minerals listed by the United States Government as "strategic" have been found in Alaska.

At present, it has not proved economical to mine these minerals. Many of the deposits are of low-grade ore. Furthermore, their inaccessibility by road and the high cost of transportation to the lower 48 states hamper development. As low-cost supplies of needed minerals used in manufacturing industries begin to run low, however, Alaska may be able to increase its production and export of minerals. Japan and the developing countries of Asia may also provide a good market. Ironically, owing to the large amount of military and domestic construction in recent years, common sand and gravel have been among the most important minerals produced in Alaska (by value).

Alaska has important deposits of the world's two most important energy fuels: coal and petroleum (along with natural gas). Incomplete geological studies have revealed that the 49th state has reserves of coal amounting to at least 100,000,000,000 tons and probably much more. Deposits of coal occur in many different locations and include several grades (lignite, subbituminous, bituminous and anthracite). Local production satisfies Alaska's need for coal, but none is exported, for mines in the lower 48 states still produce ample supplies at low cost.

On July 23, 1957, oil was struck during a drilling operation on the Kenai Peninsula. Although it was not the first discovery of petroleum in Alaska, it was the first time that oil had been found in large, commercial quantities. Since then, other wells have been brought in, including some drilled from platforms standing in Cook Inlet. Major petroleum producing companies have invested millions in the hunt for oil which has ranged far and wide over the state. Millions more will be spent in the next few years, much of it, inevitably, on dry wells.

Skagway, now a quiet town at the northern end of the Inside Passage, was once a wild frontier camp. At the height of the Klondike gold rush at the end of the 19th century, some 20,000 miners, gamblers, merchants, thieves and others crowded into the town. From Skagway, hopeful miners followed trails over White and Chilkoot Passes to the Yukon gold fields.

Young hikers climb the Forest Service trail up Mt. Roberts; the Gastineau Channel winds past far below. A bridge crossing the channel connects Juneau with Douglas Island, site of the famous Treadwell mine. In the 36 years before a disastrous cave-in closed it in 1917, the Treadwell mine produced an impressive amount of gold and paid a handsome sum in dividends to stockholders. One of the four land claims on which the mine was located cost Treadwell only $400 when purchased from the discoverer of the gold lode in 1881.

In the summer of 1969, a historic voyage took place, when the giant icebreaking oil tanker *Manhattan* (aided at one point by a smaller ice-breaking ship) successfully cut its way through the Arctic ice, on its way from New York to Prudhoe Bay. Thus, for the first time in history, a ship sailed through the Northwest Passage, a feat attempted without success by mariners since the days of Henry Hudson. This voyage proved that tankers could move oil from the North Slope to the Atlantic coast of the United States, through the polar zone. Whether this route ever becomes a reality remains to be seen. The Canadian Government indicated that it might declare the straits between its Arctic islands to be territorial waters and thus ban the passage of United States ships. The reason for this, according to conservationists, is that oil spills in cold seas might take a lifetime to disappear, creating a huge pollution problem.

However, fortunate companies are almost certain to make more important discoveries of oil and natural gas. Alaskans are benefiting in several ways from the discoveries. Anchorage already receives natural gas by pipeline from the Kenai Peninsula. Drilling operations have created jobs and business. The state treasury has benefited from fees collected for oil leases and from royalties after discoveries. In 1968, explorations on the Arctic coast revealed the presence of large petroleum deposits there.

The Arctic oil fields, in the region called the North Slope, now loom as a major element in Alaska's economy. The oil is there—the problem is getting it out. Strong opposition by conservationists and others has so far delayed construction of an 800-mile pipeline from Prudhoe Bay, on the Arctic coast, south to Valdez, on the south coast. Plans for a highway from Prudhoe Bay to the Yukon River have also been thwarted by the same groups.

The tanker "Manhattan" stuck in the solid ice of the Arctic Ocean during its historic voyage through the Northwest Passage, allowing crew members to stroll.

Oil for Alaskan markets is processed in this new refinery on the shores of the Cook Inlet about 60 miles southwest of Anchorage. Extensive exploration for petroleum is under way in the Kenai Peninsula and many other parts of the state. Alaska's first producing oil well was "brought in" in 1957.

Potatoes thrive in the fertile Matanuska Valley. The valley, which accounts for about three-fifths of the state's cultivated acreage, was opened to farming during the 1930's by pioneers brought to Alaska by the U.S. Government during the years of economic depression. Only the hardiest and most industrious farmers in the original group were successful; many went home disillusioned.

Forest rangers check a raft of logs before they are towed to the sawmill. Alaska's best commercial forests are in Tongass and Chugach National Forests, huge Government-owned preserves established at the beginning of the century. Trees are cut on a "perpetual yield" basis, so that the forest reserves will not be depleted.

AGRICULTURE AND FORESTRY

Farming in Alaska is not widespread. Currently, fewer than 20,000 acres are under cultivation, mainly in the Matanuska Valley near Anchorage and in the Tanana Valley near Fairbanks. Successful farming in Alaska requires both hard work and intelligence—and money. Long hours of toil are needed to clear land for tilling. If help must be hired, high Alaska wage rates often reduce profits. Special attention must be paid to crops because of the short growing season. In the interior, earth movements caused by melting permafrost are another danger. Because of the distances between towns and the small size of the state's population, marketing sometimes presents problems. However, Alaskan farmers receive good prices for their products since they are in competition with produce that must be imported by ship or plane from "outside" (the lower 48 states).

The great forests of southeast Alaska, under management of the U.S. Department of Agriculture, are capable of supplying many times their present yield of timber without causing any permanent harm. Alaska's forests escaped the ruinous cut-and-move-on practice of 19th-century American lumbermen, and they now stand ready to help meet the growing demand for lumber and paper pulp.

FUTURE DEVELOPMENT

In what direction Alaska will develop is not certain. The State of Alaska, according to the 1958 statehood act, can select 103,550,000 acres of vacant, unappropriated and unreserved land, and open them to the public for the purpose of establishing a wider tax base. Because wages are high, markets small, and freight charges costly, heavy industrial development in Alaska is unlikely under present circumstances. Those who support rapid industrialization and devel-

Although accounting for only a small portion of the state's total land area, southeast Alaska is the location of the state's most valuable forests. Some of the giants among the western hemlock and Sitka spruce reach heights of 175 feet and diameters of six feet. Here, lumberjacks prepare to fell a tree using a combination of hand and power woodcutting tools.

Acres and acres of hemlock pulp timber cling to the hillsides near Ketchikan, site of a gigantic new pulp mill. Alaskan timbermen are constantly looking for new markets for their products, not only in North America but also in the Far East. Japan, industrial leader of East Asia, has become a leading customer; in fact, Japanese business interests now own sawmills and pulp mills in Alaska.

Huge Alaskan king crabs are the foundation of a promising industry—crab canning. The jet age has opened new markets to the fishermen on Kodiak Island and other coastal areas, for freshly cooked crab meat can be sped to markets thousands of miles away in a few hours. Recently, Alaskan king crab fishermen have been bothered by foreign competition—Soviet trawlers operating just beyond the three-mile limit of American territorial waters.

High mountains and rushing rivers are a potential source of large quantities of hydro-electric power for Alaska. This dam is part of a project that supplies the electric power needs of the new wood pulp mill at Ketchikan. Although the facilities needed to produce hydro-electric power are usually expensive, once a project is completed the fuel—falling water—is free.

opment of the state have proposed a huge dam on the Yukon River which will generate more—and cheaper—electricity than Grand Coulee Dam and New York's Niagara power station combined. Rampart Dam, if built, would cost well over a million dollars and create a lake which, after taking 20 years to fill, would be larger than Lake Erie.

Opponents of Rampart Dam point out that it would destroy a good portion of some of Alaska's most valuable resources: scenery and wildlife. They maintain that with tourism fast becoming one of the state's leading industries—and with rapid industrialization unlikely—it would be senseless destruction of the wilderness to flood the Yukon Valley. Duck hunters in the lower 48 states have a direct stake in the issue, too, for Rampart Dam's lake would ruin one of the most important waterfowl breeding areas in North America.

The willow ptarmigan is the official bird of the state of Alaska. Here, two ptarmigan are shown in their white winter plumage. When summer comes, the white feathers turn to brown, giving the ptarmigan year-round protective camouflage. Willow ptarmigan are found in most parts of Alaska—from the Panhandle (southeastern part of the state) to the Arctic tundra in the north.